From Every Moment a Second

poems by

Robert Okaji

Finishing Line Press
Georgetown, Kentucky

From Every Moment a Second

Copyright © 2017 by Robert Okaji
ISBN 978-1-63534-331-1 First Edition
All rights reserved under International and Pan-American Copyright Conventions.
No part of this book may be reproduced in any manner whatsoever without written permission from the publisher, except in the case of brief quotations embodied in critical articles and reviews.

ACKNOWLEDGMENTS

"Magic," *Taos Journal of International Poetry & Art*
"Runaway Bus," and "What Feet Know," *Postcard Poems and Prose*
"Bottom Falling," *Into the Void*
"To the Light Entering the Shack One December Evening," *Shantih*
"The Resonance of No," *Gravel*
"Every Wind," *The Lake*
"Latitude," *Poetry Breakfast*
"On the Burden of Flowering" and "Two Cranes on a Snowy Pine (after Hokusai)," *Panoply*
"To the Lovely Green Beetles Who Carried My Notes into the Afternoon," *riverSedge*

Publisher: Leah Maines

Editor: Christen Kincaid

Cover Art: Stephanie L. Harper, https://slharperpoetry.com

Author Photo: Elizabeth Alspach

Cover Design: Elizabeth Maines McCleavy

Printed in the USA on acid-free paper.
Order online: www.finishinglinepress.com
also available on amazon.com

Author inquiries and mail orders:
Finishing Line Press
P. O. Box 1626
Georgetown, Kentucky 40324
U. S. A.

Table of Contents

Magic 1

Mayflies 2

Take Away 3

Runaway Bus 4

Bottom, Falling 5

To the Light Entering the Shack One December Evening 6

Flood Gauge in the Morning 7

The Resonance of No 8

I Have Answers 9

Every Wind 10

With No Mountain in View 11

Latitude 12

Privilege 13

What Feet Know 14

Flame 15

On the Burden of Flowering 16

If Ahead I See 17

Two Cranes on a Snowy Pine (after Hokusai) 18

Firewood 19

To the Lovely Green Beetles Who Carried My Notes
    into the Afternoon 20

Magic

You give me nothing to hold, and for this
are blessed. Devotion

is a mirror and breath, one
solid and illusory, the other
needed yet expelled, taken, dispersed.
Which begs another question
not relying on tricks.

"Who traces names on the sheets?" you ask.

I roll up my sleeves and say "Words
conceal what the night cannot."

Source becomes deed, becomes habit.
In your hand a stone, a dove, the unbroken ring.

Mayflies

Having no functioning
mouths, adults do not eat,

and live their lives
never knowing

the pleasure of food
and drink, the bitter

bite of dandelion greens
with the crisp notes

of prosecco rolling over
the tongue. Instead,

they engage in aerial
sex, often in swarms

above water, many dipping
to the surface to lay eggs,

some submerging, while
others die unfulfilled,

eaten. Who's to say
which life burns brighter;

even knowing these facts,
still I dream of flight.

Take Away

Take away the blackness,
what does night become?

Remove arugula's bitterness,
the reddened prints on a slapped
cheek, or yeast from leavened bread.

Grief enrichens no one.
The coroner's mask denies emotion.

We possess no less now than we did then.
One hand holds the root, the other, a trowel.
Soil, compost. Ash. Water, dreams. Renewal.

The economy of dying continues.

One mother stands alone, cradling pain in
both arms. The second shares her shadow.

Runaway Bus

Wishing for pristine airways
and unfeathered dreams, I lie
on my right side, and wait.

Again, the bellows flex and pump.

The relentless tickle, exploding,
another round of gasps and mucus retained,
one droplet among others,
spread across the night.

Comfort's runaway bus never slows,
and I watch it pull away, shrinking in time.

Wait, wait, I say. *I bought a ticket.*

Bottom, Falling

Through that window you see another bird
rising, unlabeled, unwanted, yet noticed.
A limb's last leaf. The boy's breath.
Like the morning after your father died,
when temperature didn't register
and heat shallowed through the morning's
end. Still you shivered. Glass. Wind.
Night's body. How to calibrate nothing's
grace? Take notes. Trace its echo. Try.

To the Light Entering the Shack One December Evening

No prayers exit here, nothing
limits you. I never knew
before.

The pear tree's ghost shudders.

Water pools in the depression of its absence.

For years I have wandered from shadow to
source, longing. Now, at rest,
you come to me and fear
evaporates. I would like to count
the smallest distraction.
I would like to disturb.

You are the name
I whisper
to clouds.

Will you leave if I open the door?

A carnival germinates in my body.

You are not death, but its closest friend.

Darkness parts, folds around you.

I close my eyes and observe.

Flood Gauge in the Morning

It reclines on its side, submerged.
So far, so good, it seems
to say. Still here, still intact.
And the bridge looks so clean
from this angle
underwater.

I toss
a fist-size stone
onto the upstream
side of the road,
and watch it wash away.
Maybe we'll cross tomorrow.

The Resonance of No

Yes, yes, we've heard. The dishwasher wastes less
and cleans better. But Kenkō believed in the beauty
of leisure, and how better to make nothing
while standing with hands in soapy water, thoughts
skipping from Miles Davis's languid notes to the spider
ascending to safe shelter under the sill (after I blow
on her to amuse myself), washing my favorite knife
and wondering if I should hone it, not to mention
my skills on the six-string or the potato peeler.
And if I linger at the plates, even the chipped one,
admiring their gleam after hot water rinses away
the soap residue, who could question the quick gulp
of ale or the shuffle of an almost-but-not-quite
dance step-or-stumble while arranging them on the
ribbed rack, back-to-back, in time to Coltrane's
solo. Then the forgotten food processor's blade
bites my palm, and I remember that I've outgrown
the dark suit, the cut branches still need bundling
and none of the words I've conjured and shaped
over decades and miles will extend their comfort
when I stand at my father's grave this week or next.

I Have Answers

But the questions remain.

A little pepper, some salt,
butter. Our rosemary needs pruning
and the music's too loud

to hear. The lizard basks in sunlight
eight minutes old, but I forget to ask

what else we need. Or want. *Just this,*
she says. *Red, like your favorite sky,*

the in-between, the misplaced one.

Every Wind

Every wind loses itself,
no matter where

it starts. I want
a little piece of you.

No.

I want your atmosphere
bundled in a small rice paper packet
and labeled with strings of new rain
and stepping stones.

I want
the grace of silence
blowing in through the cracked
window, disturbing only
the shadows.

Everywhere I go, bits of me linger,
searching for you.

Grief ages one thread at a time,

lurking like an odor
among the lost
things,

or your breath,
still out there,

drifting.

With No Mountain in View

Like a mirage, you shift ever forward,
blonde hair concealing your eyes, one
long leg draped over the chair's arm,
a reminder of inconstancy and promises
constructed to collapse. Such power,
such wisdom, at seventeen.
Through the window I see
horses in the paddock, a lone
figure by the road, and steam
rising from the earth. Your voice,
as it was, and mine, as it never sounded,
merged only in fantasy. Something
crumbles at the edge. A crow flaps away.

Latitude

Sometimes it's enough to know
that a chicken preceded this egg,

that some crossed the Atlantic,
and others, yes, the road. Perhaps

I am too enamored of this fondness
for imprecision, never certain where

evening ends in your latitude,
where morning begins in mine,

but I've come to appreciate, late in
life, the finer points of egg cookery,

the beauty of basting with olive
oil, three ways of poaching,

and the tender art of scrambling.
This is of course metaphor, and

not. The truth is seldom so simply
derived. You hold the egg. I

offer salt. Your pan. My butter.
We both bring the heat.

Privilege

Every hour becomes another.

Surrendering minutes, accepting
gain, which gravities restrain us?

Strong coffee, books. A smile.

Such imponderables—the measured
digit, starlife, an unmarked sheet of
paper fluttering to the floor.

Sometimes the lights go out
and we wonder when they'll return,
not if. Or the laborer misinterprets
a statement and stains the carpet.

There but for the grace...
Anything can happen, and frequently does,

but we open the door and step out, unhindered.

What Feet Know

The earth and its subterfuge.
Gravity and the points between here and there.

And sometimes the rasp of grainy mud
clenched between toes,
or a rock under the arch,
an explanation too pointed
for display on a page,
too hard, too much for flesh to bear.

No constellations foment underground.
Nothing there orbits a companion.

No light but for that darkness the heel scrapes away.

Flame

Drifting, she passes through the frame.

Reshapes borders, edges.

The way smoke scribes a letter in the sky with
gases and particulates. Intractable. Impermanent.

But not like a risen corpse
yet to accept its body's stilling, or
the flooded creek's waters taking
a house and the family within. Some things

are explainable. This morning you drained
the sink, and thunder set off a neighbor's alarm.

From every moment, a second emerges.

Picture a man lighting a candle where a home once stood.

On the Burden of Flowering

Even the cactus wren
surrenders itself
to the task,

though it rarely listens
to my voice. How do clouds
blossom day to day

and leave so little
behind? The bookless shelf
begs to be filled, but instead

I watch the morning age
as the sun arcs higher.
Yesterday you said

the mint marigold
was dying. Today it
stands tall. Yellowing.

If Ahead I See

Gray skies filtered through light,
eyes adapting space,
the possibilities of the

horizon or a foot
lashing out in reflex,
what do I learn?

The house finch sings as if
all air will expire at song's end.

Falling, I release this misplaced trust.
The path, muddied and crowded with fools.

Two Cranes on a Snowy Pine (after Hokusai)

Who knows where bird
begins and tree

ends,

which branch shifts
snow, which bears

eternity. This, too, will share

joy,
elusive green

and breath,
with no thought

of flight

and night's
fall.

Firewood

For two years the oak
loomed, leafless.
We had aged
together, but somehow
I survived the drought
and ice storms, the
regret and wilt,
the explosions within,
and it did not.

I do not know
the rituals of trees,
how they mourn
a passing, or if
the sighs I hear
betray only my own
frailties, but even
as I fuel the saw and
tighten the chain,
I look carefully
for new growth.

To the Lovely Green Beetles Who Carried My Notes into the Afternoon

Such beauty should not be bound,
thus I tied loose knots,

knowing you would slip free
and shed my words

as they were meant,
across browned lawns,

just over the cedar fence
or at the curb's edge,

never to be assembled,
and better for it.

The son of a career soldier, **Robert Okaji** moved from place to place throughout his childhood. He holds a BA in history from The University of Texas at Austin, served without distinction in the U.S. Navy, lived the hand-to-mouth existence of a bookstore owner, and worked in a library and as a university administrator. He lives in Texas with his wife, two dogs, some books and a beverage refrigerator stocked with craft beer.

He has never been awarded a literary prize, but at age seven won a rolling trashcan cart that's still in use.

Recent publications include the chapbook *If Your Matter Could Reform* (Dink Press), two micro-chapbooks, *You Break What Falls* and *No Eye but the Moon's: Adaptations from the Chinese* (Origami Poems Project), a mini-digital chapbook, *Interval's Night* (Platypus Press), and "The Circumference of Other," a collection appearing in *Ides: A Collection of Poetry Chapbooks* (Silver Birch Press). His work has appeared in *Taos Journal of International Poetry & Art, Boston Review, Hermeneutic Chaos, Glass: A Journal of Poetry, Panoply, Eclectica, Clade Song, Into the Void, High Window, West Texas Literary Review* and elsewhere. Visit his blog, *O at the Edges*, at http://robertokaji.com/.

www.ingramcontent.com/pod-product-compliance
Lightning Source LLC
LaVergne TN
LVHW041525070426
835507LV00013B/1828